To BRIAN

Best Wishes Always —

Charlie Meacham

Praise for *Arnie and Jack*

I can say with complete conviction that there isn't a person, past or present, who knows more about Arnold Palmer and Jack Nicklaus, and the stories that took place between the two of us — and individually — than Charlie Mechem.
Jack Nicklaus

There can never be enough stories about these two great legends from the game of golf. Charlie has captured and told us some of the best.
Tom Watson

I am a big fan of Charlie Mechem! I lived some of the history recorded in Charlie's wonderful book, but it was great to learn so much more. Charlie was such a true friend to both Arnold and Jack, and the book really puts you in the same room with them. It made me chuckle. It's a wonderful trip down golf's memory lane. If you love golf, which so many of us do, this book will be one of your favorites.
Nancy Lopez

Charlie was leading the LPGA when I became the PGA Tour's commissioner, and I had many opportunities to listen to his stories about Arnie and Jack. This enjoyable book details some of those and many others as he recounts his relationship with two legends of the game; actually three — if you count Charlie.
Tim Finchem, former PGA Tour Commissioner

Charlie is one of the best storytellers ever. This book shares his experiences — inside and outside the ropes — with many of the game's most beloved personalities, including Arnie and Jack. Charlie's writing touches every emotion — you'll have some laughs and you'll also shed some tears. Like golf, life has ups and downs, and he beautifully paints that picture in his own unique way.
Annika Sorenstam

Charlie Mechem, like the two subjects of this book, is an American golf treasure. When he grabs his hat (which we hope will be a long while yet) we should have him stuffed and mounted in the World Golf Hall of Fame.
David Feherty

Not too many people were in the inner circle of Jack Nicklaus and Arnold Palmer, but Charlie Mechem was right there. Charlie is the only person who can tell these incredible stories of golf, life and friendship with Jack and Arnie, and he's given us a real gift by sharing his memories with all of us.
Juli Inkster

Charlie Mechem shares his uniquely special place in both the professional and personal lives of two titans of golf in *Arnie and Jack*. An easy read that will give you an inside look at their relationship, one filled with competitive admiration and love of the game.
Dottie Pepper

Charlie Mechem has many gifts, the greatest among them being his genius for true friendship. His warm, revealing, and astute reflections from his long friendships with two giants are now a gift to golf history.
Jaime Diaz, Golf Channel analyst

Charlie Mechem wasn't there at the Separation of the Continents, but he showed up shortly thereafter and he's been in the room when all the important stuff happened since. His friendship with Jack and Arnie gives him an insight into golf unmatched by anyone today. My only criticism of his book is it's not long enough — I always want to hear more Charlie stories.
Jerry Tarde, Editor-in-Chief, *Golf Digest*

ARNIE AND JACK

STORIES OF MY LONG FRIENDSHIP WITH TWO REMARKABLE MEN

CHARLES S. MECHEM JR.

WITH FOREWORDS BY JACK NICKLAUS AND DOC GIFFIN

MISSION POINT PRESS

Arnie and Jack: Stories of My Long Friendship with Two Remarkable Men

By Charles S. Mechem Jr.

Mission Point Press

2554 Chandler Road

Traverse City, Michigan 49696

www.MissionPointPress.com

231-421-9513

Cover and book design by Sarah Meiers

Printed in the United States of America

ISBN: 978-1-954786-78-3

Library of Congress Control Number: 2022902836

FOREWORD BY JACK NICKLAUS

Photo by Jim Mandeville/
Nicklaus Companies

Much like a four-leaf clover, a friend is hard to find and lucky to have. Truly great friends are difficult to leave and impossible to forget. There are two people among those who have been like four-leaf clovers to me — Arnold Palmer and Charlie Mechem. Arnold and I were fierce competitors, but more important, we were friends for 60 years. And then there is Charlie, who has been a dear friend of mine for over 50 years. Charlie was a trusted companion and advisor of Arnold's for more than 20 years, sharing an office with Arnold at the Bay Hill Club in Orlando. I can say with complete conviction that there isn't a person, past or present, who knows more about Arnold Palmer and Jack Nicklaus, and the stories that took place between the two of us — and individually — than Charlie Mechem.

William Shakespeare, the rare person I could mention whose work is actually older than Charlie and me, once wrote that a friend is one who knows you as you are, understands where you have been, accepts what you have become, and still gently allows you to grow.

Aside from being one of the best friends I have had in the world, Charlie is a brilliant man, a great contributor to the game of golf, and someone I have always viewed as a trusted confidant in business and in life. Actually, Charlie has meant so much to everyone's life he has touched. My wife Barbara and I, as well as our sizable family, feel blessed to be counted among those he has forever impacted.

The book you are about to read comes from one of the kindest, most sincere men I have ever met. He is someone who would never tell a story that would harm a soul, but will share a story to certainly touch your soul. Charlie's book is full of great stories and wisdom all delivered with his unshakable wit, aplomb, and class. I hope you enjoy it. Actually, I know you will enjoy it!

FOREWORD BY DOC GIFFIN

In some ways, Charlie Mechem's interesting book takes the words right out of my mouth.

Many of the observations that Charlie makes coincide with the thoughts and opinions I might have expressed, had I decided to write a similar book about my 50 years with Arnold Palmer. For all those years, I was within shouting distance of my boss and close friend during the six warm Pennsylvania months every year and just a phone call away the rest of the time. For a decade or so in Charlie's case, he was little more than arm's length away from him at Bay Hill during the other six months and in constant touch during the remaining years he was with us.

Arnold had excellent advisors within his organization, but he also treasured the counsel he solicited from Charlie and from longer range — several other business executive/close friends — over the years. Although his association with Arnold was for a shorter time, Charlie and I were in that unique position to form opinions from our up-close-and-personal association with this great man. Those seem to me to carry more weight than those of others drawn from a more distant range.

Of particular interest, Charlie deals with the questions that have been so often asked of both of us: Were Arnie and Jack really friends? In a word — yes — and he elaborates, making a salient point that this was bulwarked by the close friendship that existed between Barbara Nicklaus and Winnie Palmer through all the years up to Winnie's passing in 1999. He hit the nail on the head in both regards. The two men could not have had two more supportive and admired wives.

I smiled as I was reminded while reading this book by some of the things that he pointed out that were typical Arnold Palmer. Particularly amusing is the vignette in which he relates, as an example of the differences that certainly existed between these two iconic athletes, how each spent a normal day in their latter-day lives. Humorous, too, is Charlie's account of how he cajoled the two of them into co-designing the impressive The King & The Bear golf course at the World Golf Hall of Fame in Florida. (It was the only one they co-designed, although they later teamed up with their mutual Big Three friend, Gary Player, to create the 27-hole Champions Retreat at Augusta, Georgia.)

Charlie also reminds us of the glowing tribute Jack paid when Arnold received the Congressional Medal of Honor in the Capitol Rotunda.

Lest this seem a bit one-sided, I want you to know that I found the many anecdotes Charlie relates about his much longer association with Jack equally interesting and entertaining. Obviously, Jack has had the same high regard for Charlie Mechem as Arnold had.

Charlie concludes his introduction to this collection of his memories of his friendship with Arnie and Jack by saying:

"I hope you will enjoy."

You will.

ACKNOWLEDGEMENTS

Marilyn and Charlie

First to my executive assistant, Gretlyn Thomas, and her assistant, Carolyn Heineman, who handled the heavy work for this book. My practice is to dictate to Gretlyn or Carolyn, they transcribe my dictation, and then I edit it. They are both excellent at what they do, and it is no exaggeration to say this book would not exist without their expert help.

Next, to my friends, Russ Meyer and Gary Singer, both of whom contributed significantly to the stories in this book.

Thanks also to Arnie's good friend Howdy Giles and to Reade Tilley for their help in securing photographs.

And, lastly, but not "leastly" to Marilyn, my long-suffering wife of some 70 years. She has supported me in all my many ventures and has contributed beyond description to my successes, and she has always stood by me in my failures. With this book, like others I have written, I have read the manuscript to her word for word and her comments were always excellent and her critique always on point. I owe her the deepest debt of thanks for this and for so many other things too numerous to mention.

Arnie and Jack line up a putt during the Ryder Cup playoffs at Muirfield in Gullane, East Lothian, Scotland, in 1973. Nicklaus and Palmer were teamed together against Peter Townsend and Harry Bannerman of Great Britain. *Photo from the Bettmann Collection via Getty Images*

TABLE OF CONTENTS

INTRODUCTION

I would like to explain the origin of this book about Arnie and Jack.

I am a member of the Tradition Golf Club in La Quinta, California. Arnie designed the golf course at Tradition and had a seasonal home there. My wife Marilyn and I lived next door to Arnie and his wife, Kit, at Tradition and enjoyed many happy times together. Some months ago, the president of the club said to me: "Charlie, you may be one of the few people who knew both Jack and Arnie intimately over a period of years. I would like you to

Arnie, Charlie and Jack. We were all together for a memorial service for a mutual friend in La Quinta, California.

make a talk to the membership of the club about that very special relationship. I am sure you have a lot of Jack and Arnie stories." I said I would be delighted, and this book is my effort to recreate the talk that I gave.

I received a surprise validation of my relationships with Arnie and Jack at Jack's Memorial Tournament in Dublin, Ohio, in 2021. I was speaking to Jack about what the club president said to me, and when I mentioned it was suggested that I was one of the few people who knew both Arnie and him intimately over a long period of time, Jack looked at me and held up his index finger. "You were No. 1," he said. Obviously, I was deeply flattered, and that has given me even greater impetus to tell the stories in this book.

I should note that some of what's here are individual stories about Arnie or Jack; some are stories about the two of them together. I think these recollections combine to give you a unique view of two of the most unforgettable people I have ever known.

In 2013, I wrote and published a book called *Who's That With Charlie?* It was not a memoir, but rather a collection of memories and reminisces of my times with many good friends, obviously including Arnie and Jack. I repeat some of the stories from that book here, but since it has now been nine years since I wrote it, I think some of the stories are well worth repeating.

A final word of explanation: There is no sequence or chronological order to these stories. They took place in various locations and at various times. Basically, the only order is how I remember them. I hope you will enjoy.

DOC GIFFIN

AS YOU WILL HAVE NOTED, one of the forewords to this book was written by a gentleman named Doc Giffin.* Doc was gracious enough to agree to write the foreword, and it occurred to me that I should say a word or two about him since his name may not be familiar to many of you. Doc was born, fittingly, in western Pennsylvania not far from Arnold Palmer's home in Latrobe. He attended the University of Pittsburgh, where he became enamored of the writing business. He served as the sports editor and later as the editor proper of his college newspaper, *The Pitt News*. Doc later joined *The Pittsburgh Press*, where he got to know the legendary Bob Drum, a brilliant and larger-than-life character who served as the golf editor. As an aside, Bob Drum was probably the first person to realize that a young golfer from Latrobe, Pennsylvania, was destined for greater things.

It was Drum who, when learning that the PGA Tour had offered Doc the job as the tour press secretary in 1962, encouraged Doc to take the job. Doc was 33 years old at the time.

Arnie asked Doc to join him in 1966, and he served as his personal assistant for the rest of Arnie's life. The precise date that Doc joined Arnie was July 24, 1966.

I used to tease Arnie by telling him that he couldn't utter a word or a sentence that wasn't written or conceived by Doc. That, of course, was not

---

* Doc's given name was Donald W. Giffin but frankly I had never heard this until I began writing this book. To everyone he was "Doc."

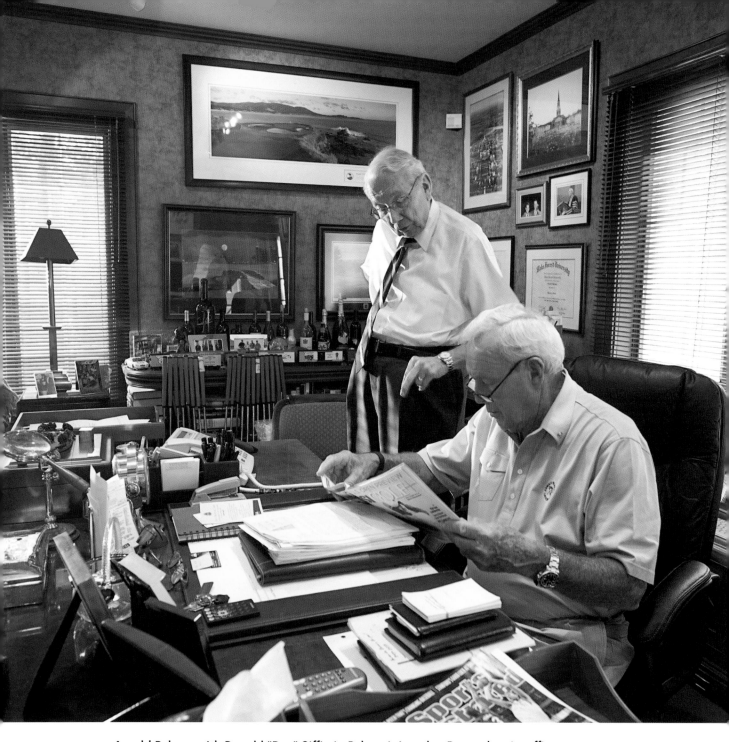

Arnold Palmer with Donald "Doc" Giffin in Palmer's Latrobe, Pennsylvania, office. Giffin had been Palmer's executive assistant since 1966. *Photo by Fred Vuich / Sports Illustrated via Getty Images*

"Doc's real title should be 'friend' or 'everlasting friend.' Someone you can trust with your life."

true. Arnie was an extremely articulate guy, and Doc was able to capture Arnie's thoughts and ideas in an amazing way. In an article by Tom Callahan (a fine writer in his own right) in a recent Golf Digest, Tom quoted Doc as follows: "I was never Arnold's handler. He didn't need a handler. People ask me why is Arnold Palmer so popular? The answer is simple. He likes people and they know it. His public face and private face are exactly the same."

When asked what Doc's title was, Arnold said, "Doc's real title should be 'friend' or 'everlasting friend.' Someone you can trust with your life."

During my years with Arnie, I got to know Doc very well and we have become good friends. He truly is a remarkable man, a superb writer, and it's almost impossible to imagine Arnie without him. Happily, that never was necessary.

Perhaps it is most fitting that the Bay Hill Media Center (which is used extensively during the Arnold Palmer Invitational) was named in his honor. It is now and will always be known as the "Doc Giffin Media Center."

I could go on and on, but there is no need. I have enormous respect for Doc Giffin and am deeply honored that he agreed to write one of the forewords to this book.

THE BEGINNING

As I began my speech to the members of Tradition, I asked if they could hear me from the podium without a microphone. When I brought this up, I was reminded of a very funny story that Jack told me.

When Arnie was awarded the Congressional Gold Medal at the U.S. Capitol building in Washington in 2012, Jack was there (as was I), and Jack and a number of politicos made very warm speeches. Arnie listened to the speeches quietly and without emotion. I noticed this, as did Jack, and Jack and I both agreed this was not like Arnie. After the ceremony, Jack went over and asked, "Arnie, could you hear anything those people were saying?" And Arnie said, "Zero." Arnie's partial deafness was legendary.

I then told the audience at Tradition that I'd learned that there were several ways to begin a speech. One of my favorites goes like this, "Folks, we each have a job to do today. My job is to speak. Your job is to listen. If you finish your job before I finish mine, please raise your hand!" This got a laugh, and I moved forward with my talk with everybody in a good mood. Since this is a book, not a speech, I need to revise this line a bit to say, "Your job is to read this book. My job is to make it interesting enough that you will want to read it." Unfortunately, if you raise your hand to indicate that you do not enjoy the book, I will not be able to see you, but you will have the comfort of knowing that you have expressed your negative feelings. I truly hope that will not be necessary.

I was blessed, and I really mean that with a capital "B," to get to know both Jack and Arnie very well. And, it has always been a measure of pride

Arnie receives the Congressional Gold Medal from Speaker of the House John Boehner.
Photo by Howdy Giles.

for me to have been able to watch and listen to the two of them — in some ways very different, in some ways very similar, but always interesting and fun to be around. They were similar in their code of ethics, their loyalties, the way they felt the game should be played, the importance of respect for other people — they were dead on. But in other ways, they were very different. For example, Jack was a great lover of sports of many kinds. Arnie could

Arnie also received the Presidential Medal of Freedom, the nation's highest civil award, from President George W. Bush in 2004. *Photo by Luke Frazza/AFP via Getty Images.*

have played any sport he wanted to and excel at it, I'm sure, but he didn't care about that. He only wanted to play golf. Golf was his life. Jack loved baseball, and all reports are that he was a great catcher. He said if he had not gone into golf, he'd have gone into baseball. He was a switch-hitter/catcher — a rare combination. He was also a great hunter. And a great deep-sea fisherman. In fact, in 1978, Jack landed a 1,358-pound marlin while fishing off the Great Barrier Reef in Australia. That's a lot of fish folks. That's a lot of marlin!!

I thought it might be helpful to recount how I met each of them for the first time. Not surprisingly, the experiences were quite different.

MEETING JACK

I'LL START WITH JACK BECAUSE I MET HIM FIRST. The company that I ran in Cincinnati, Ohio, Taft Broadcasting Company, commissioned Jack to build a golf course on a piece of land that we owned north of the city. That was in 1970, and he was just getting started with his course design efforts. Of course, he was already famous and an Ohio guy. So he was the obvious choice to design the course. It was a public golf course, and he did a great job.

When he was finished, we were having a drink to celebrate. We chatted.

"Jack, you've done a superb job," I said.

"Charlie, I'm happy with it," he replied. "In fact, we're going to have a PGA Tournament here next year."

I was absolutely stunned. "What?!"

Jack repeated, "We're going to have a PGA Tournament here next year."

"Jack, come on! It's a public course, the trees are whips, the grass is barely growing."

"Charlie, let me tell you something. Beman owes me one, and we're going to have a tournament." Deane Beman was then commissioner of the PGA Tour.

"Is the course going to be able to handle that?" I asked.

"Charlie, let me tell you something else. You can make any course tournament ready if you make the greens lightning fast, grow the rough, and narrow the fairways."

And he was right. Guess what happened? The winner of the first tournament was Jack Nicklaus! The subsequent winners were Ben Crenshaw, Mike

Sinking a winning putt with Dinah Shore at Jack's golf course in Cincinnati.
She was an unforgettable person.

Hill (Mike Hill was not as well known, but he was great player), and a guy named Miller Barber.

If you don't know the name Miller Barber, Google him and you will have fun reading about him. He was one of a kind. He didn't look like a golfer, but he could really play, which he demonstrated both on the PGA Tour and on the Senior Champions Tour later (originally called the Senior Tour). But he was also kind of a mystery guy. He once said, "You know, I'm not married, so I don't want anybody to know where I'm going at night, but I'll be fine." So, the players started calling him "Mr. X," and he always went by "Mr. X."

So those were the four winners. The fact that they were all great players proved Jack's point — the course was tough enough!

As the years went by, my involvement with Jack, and my company's involvement with Jack, increased. One of the most notable accomplishments was the production of the video of Jack's matchless book — *Golf My Way*. Discussions had developed because Taft Broadcasting had a division (WorldVision) that had the ability and expertise to produce a video version. Also, the head of our WorldVision Division was a fellow named Kevin O'Sullivan who was an avid golfer and worshipped Jack Nicklaus. Working with Ken Bowden of the Nicklaus organization, Worldvison produced a superb video version of the book. And we were now ready to discuss marketing and distribution.

I remember vividly a meeting in New York City in which we discussed the production and sale of the video. One of the principal issues was what price it should be. Most instructional videos at that time were $30 or $40 and we naturally were thinking along those lines. Then Jack spoke up and, as always, we all listened! He said he thought we should price it significantly higher than other golf videos then on the market. His point was that it was a premier product and should be priced as such. So, with some trepidation but with full confidence in Jack's view, we priced it (as I remember) at just under $100. The video was and still is the best instructional video ever made. It sold extremely well. As others have noted, it was responsible for millions

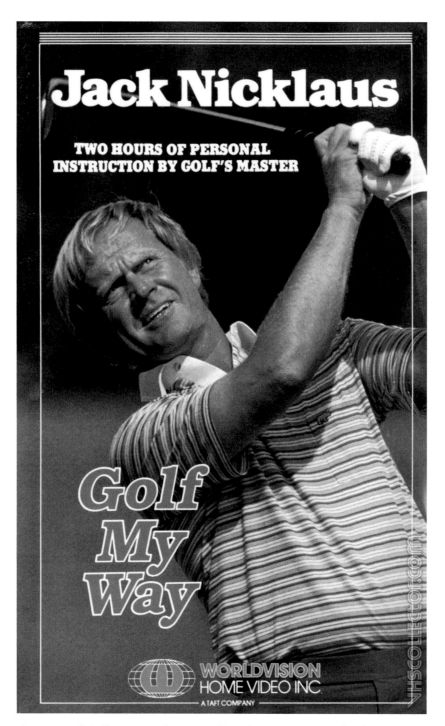

The cover of Golf My Way, the groundbreaking instructional video that Taft Broadcasting made with Jack.

A great product deserves a strong price and to price it any other way tends to give the public a distorted view of its worth.

of golfers learning and/or improving their golf game. It will always be a fitting tribute to Jack's skill and ability to communicate his thoughts about the game.

There is a broader lesson here and it has served me well in a number of instances throughout the years. That lesson is to understand that a great product deserves a strong price and to price it any other way tends to give the public a distorted view of its worth. In a totally different context, I learned this lesson once again. We made a corporate decision in 1982 to keep Taft Broadcasting Company's Kings Island amusement park open during the Christmas season. This was a unique decision that proved to be quite successful. However, when we were meeting to decide what the entrance fee should be, a debate ensued with some of the group arguing that, since we were not sure how attractive the product would be, we should charge nothing — make entrance to the park gratis. The counter argument was that this would cheapen the product and people would assume that we were charging nothing because we weren't confident of the experience. This latter argument carried the day and we ended up charging (if memory serves me) $10 or so and, as I noted, it was a great success. After a few years of hiatus, I understand that the park is once again opening at Christmas time.

Important postscript. Since writing this I have run across a letter from Jack, dated March 15, 1987, that speaks loudly to the success of the video.

Here's the letter:

Jack Nicklaus

March 5, 1987

Dear Charlie:

    I'm absolutely overwhelmed by the success GOLF MY WAY has enjoyed. Each time you send me another check, I can't believe my eyes! I know I'm repeating myself, but I wanted to tell you again how delighted I am that this worked out so well for us both.

    Thanks again for the very generous check. I look forward to seeing you at the Partnership meeting next month, if not sooner.

Best regards,

Mr. Charles S. Mechem, Jr.
Chairman of the Board
TAFT BROADCASTING COMPANY
1718 Young Street
Cincinnati, Ohio   45210

/mk

A VERY FUNNY PICTURE-TAKING EXPERIENCE

THE "PARTNERSHIP" OF COMPANIES THAT JACK REFERS TO in his letter is a reference to an event that he and Barbara had each year at their home in Florida for Jack's business partners. These were people and companies that did business with the Nicklaus Companies. Taft Broadcasting was one of these companies, and Marilyn and I attended the dinner whenever we could.

At one such affair, Taft Broadcasting was honored as "Partner of the Year," and I received a very nice plaque and silver trophy recognizing our efforts. After dinner, Barb pulled Jack and me aside and said, "I want to get a picture of you two holding the trophy," but then Barb said, "I don't know where I put my camera. I am never without my camera, but I simply can't find it." She looked around and spotted another guest who had a camera.

Barbara persuaded the man to take a picture of Jack and me, even though he spoke no English. As Jack and I posed for the picture, holding the trophy, another gentleman stepped into the picture with us. As politely as we could, we tried to make him understand that only Jack and I should be in this particular picture. He stepped aside, but the man with the camera shook his head and refused to take the picture unless and until the other gentleman was part of it. It soon became clear that the picture was not going to be taken unless all three of us were in it. The three of us posed and the picture was taken. When that was accomplished, the man with the camera was happy to take a picture of Jack and I together holding the trophy. The puzzle of the third man was solved before the evening ended.

It turned out that the "third man" was the boss of the man with the camera, and the man with the camera was not about to take a picture of Jack Nicklaus that didn't include his boss! As far as he was concerned, I was not even there! On my office wall, to this day, are both pictures — one with Jack and one with our new friend with the trophy. We both laugh as we remember what it took to get the photograph made! I smile again each time I view these two pictures side by side.

Taft Broadcasting and Jack Nicklaus worked together on many projects.

The photograph with the borrowed camera.

JACK'S STUNNING ADVICE TO ME

BEFORE I MET ARNIE, I was asked to become commissioner of the LPGA. Here is one of my favorite stories about a meeting with Jack. When asked to become the commissioner, I thought, *I know a lot about the golf world, but I don't know everything. I probably ought to go down and see Nicklaus and just ask him if he thinks I'm doing the right thing.* So, I went down to his office in North Palm Beach to discuss the matter with him.

"Jack," I said, "the LPGA has asked me to be its commissioner. I'm inclined to do it, but what do you think?"

Jack said, "You better damn well do it. I recommended you."

Absolutely, cross my heart, I had no idea! What had happened was that the head of the LPGA Players Association, Judy Dickinson, was a very close friend of Jack's. Judy was also the wife of Gardner Dickinson, the great pro golfer, who many of you will remember. Judy apparently asked Jack if he knew anybody who should be approached regarding the LPGA commissioner position, and that's when he recommended me.

I was obviously very proud of his recommendation. I decided to accept the job.

MEETING ARNIE

NOW, LET'S TALK ABOUT HOW I CAME TO KNOW ARNIE. My last tournament as commissioner of the LPGA in late 1995 was a team event at PGA West. I noticed that Jack and Arnie were paired together. So, I went down to the first tee to wish them well. I didn't know Arnie that well at that point. I had spent only casual time with him during my LPGA days. He said, "I've been meaning to call you. Let's have a beer after my round." I was somewhat surprised, but obviously agreed.

After he finished his round, we went up into the dining room and bar at PGA West and, in typical Arnie fashion, he ordered for each of us. Then, without any warmup to the topic, said, "I want you to come in and run all my companies."

Well, after I picked myself up off the floor, I said, "Arnie, I'm overwhelmed, I'm obviously flattered, but I can't do it."

"What do you mean, you can't do it?" he asked, surprised.

"Well, I've already made commitments to several companies back in Cincinnati to become chairman of their corporate boards, and with those kinds of responsibilities, I can't commit to a full-time job."

"I understand," Arnie said. "But we need to figure out something."

I agreed. "I would really like to find a way to make it work," I said.

About two or three months later, he called me. We were then living in south Florida. "I've got an idea," he said. "Why don't you come up to Bay Hill and we'll visit."

The Bay Hill Club in Orlando was Arnie's principal home and business office during the winter months. Marilyn and I drove up for dinner and met

Iconic statue of Arnie near the first tee at the Bay Hill Club. *Photo by Matt Majka*

with Arnie and Winnie[1], as well as Russ Meyer, one of Arnie's dearest and closest friends, and his wife Helen.[2] We had dinner and a very pleasant conversation. The next morning. Arnie and I met in his office and he said, "I've got an idea. Why don't you just act as my personal advisor and consultant.[3] That way you will have time to handle your other commitments and still help me." I said, "Sounds great to me."

He then added, "There are only two conditions. One, you and Marilyn have to move to Bay Hill. Second, I want you in this office right here," pointing to an office just a few feet away from his desk. He said, "That's your office."

Let me explain a little more about the office where I was destined to spend most of the next 10 years of my life. Arnie's office adjoined a slightly smaller office, which had a door between them. The desk behind which I would soon sit was about six or seven feet from Arnie's desk. During those years, that door was virtually never closed, and we could easily communicate from our respective desks. We not only could communicate vocally through the door, but Arnie would frequently throw a letter or some other piece of correspondence through the door and say, "What do you think of this?"

I did not learn until much later why Arnie approached me. It turns out that his delightful and talented wife, Winnie, had spoken with Arnie on several occasions, to the effect that if he predeceased her, she wanted him to have somebody to act as a "go between" with IMG, Mark McCormack's worldwide sports marketing firm, whose first client was Arnie. She was friendly

---

(1) Winnie was Arnie's first wife, a very special and remarkable person who tragically passed away on Nov. 20, 1999.

(2) I should note that Russ Meyer is widely respected and known as the finest private-aircraft executive in the world. He and Arnie met early in their respective careers and bonded immediately because of their interest in flying and golf. Russ and I have become very close friends.

(3) Arnie often jokingly referred to me as "his lawyer," even though I had not practiced law for quite a few years.

Arnie views the 18th hole at Bay Hill during the first round of the 2013 Arnold Palmer Invitational. *Photo by David Cannon via Getty Images*

with Mark and his associates, but said she would be more comfortable with somebody who spoke "their language."

Long before our dinner at Bay Hill, I had been asked by my dear friend, Joe Gibbs, to be one of the speakers at the formal launch of his Golf Channel. At dinner, I was seated next to Winnie, and though at that time I had never met her, I don't think I ever bonded with anyone more quickly. We had many

A beautiful aerial view of the lodge and
a portion of the golf course at Bay Hill.
Photo by Matt Majka

common interests, and I knew we would become good friends. Apparently when Arnie and Winnie got home that night, Winnie mentioned her discussion with me and said something to the effect that, "Charlie is the kind of person that I have been urging you to associate with who could be helpful to me should you predecease me."

And that is how it all began.

The famous Rolex clock at Bay Hill. *Photo by Matt Majka*

MY DEAL
WITH ARNIE

THERE WAS AN UNUSUAL ASPECT to my relationship with Arnold. When we first agreed that I would be his advisor and consultant, we also agreed on a generous monthly stipend. In the next few weeks, I decided that I was not comfortable with this. So, I went into Arnie's office and said, "Arnie, I have thought about this a lot. I don't want you to pay me anything." He looked

One of my favorite pictures with Arnie. He wrote on it:
"To Charlie, 'my man.'"

at me with surprise and said, "No one ever asked me to not pay them! Why not?" I replied, "As I thought about it, I began to realize that if you pay me, then I am an employee. Maybe a different kind of employee, but nonetheless an employee. If I work with you as a friend without pay, I think I can probably be more direct and open with you and you can better accept and respect my advice. I will simply be more comfortable." Arnie said, "I completely understand and agree — that's the way it will be."

As I have thought back on this decision over the years, I have become more and more convinced that I did the right thing. To be totally fair, I should note that I was able to use my office to transact other "non-Palmer" business and that could be considered a form of compensation. The point of this comment is that I received no compensation from Arnie and that had a very significant effect on our relations.

A TYPICAL DAY
AT BAY HILL

THIS WAS THE BEGINNING of one of the happiest times in our lives. On a typical day, I would arrive at the office around 8 a.m. More often than not, Arnie was already there or he was having breakfast in the downstairs dining room. We would work until around noon and then have lunch. Typically,

One of the side benefits of knowing Arnie was getting to know his friends. In this snapshot, Arnie and I are with Russ Meyer, at left. Russ was perhaps Arnold's oldest and closest friend, sharing common interests in golf and aviation. *Photo by Howdy Giles*

Arnie would then either hit balls or play in the notorious Bay Hill Shootout. (The Shootout is legendary in golf circles. It is a special competition that takes place every day at Bay Hill. It is much too complicated to explain here. Just google "Bay Hill Club Shootout" to get the full story). After lunch, I would go back to the office and work until mid-afternoon.

I would then typically go home and, more often than not, Marilyn and I would play some golf either by ourselves or with some of our friends.

That was it! Not bad, eh?

Another friend of Arnie's, Dick Ferris, center, is in this picture and we are enjoying a good time together. Dick was one of Arnold's best friends. Dick was CEO of United Airlines and served as chairman of the PGA Policy Board for many years. Sadly, Dick passed away on Jan. 17, 2022. *Photo by Howdy Giles*

Jack clearing a bunker at The Bears Club. *Photo by Jim Mandeville/ Nicklaus Companies*

JACK JOINS THE PGA TOUR

I SUSPECT THAT MANY OF YOU READERS are too young to remember the early days when Jack first came on Tour and began to challenge Arnie. Those of you who do remember will recall that it was not pleasant. In fact, it was just plain ugly. Much of the crowd — the famed Arnie's Army — was against him. If Jack would hit a poor shot (which didn't happen often, but it did happen), the crowd would applaud. Or they would yell "Fat Jack" or some other derogatory comment. You should know that at that time Jack was over-weight, he had a "burr" haircut, and wore a pork pie hat! (Such hats are round with a turned-up brim and a flat crown.) Arnie never encouraged or condoned the bad language from the crowds, and Jack performed as though he didn't even hear it. He played right through it. In fact, he had the most incredible concentration of any golfer I've ever known, although Tiger Woods would be a very close second.

I learned about his power of concentration very early on. The first deal I made with Jack was in Jacksonville, Florida, where he was playing a tournament. We had dinner, drinks, and signed an agreement. (These many years later, I don't remember the substance of the agreement). We were probably together four or five hours. The next day, I went out to the course and positioned myself on the walkway from the green (where Jack was holing out) to the next tee. He came off the green, walked right beside me, looked at me, and walked right on. I was like, "What's going on?"

When I saw one of his buddies a little later on, I said, "Did I do something to irritate Jack? He looked me straight in the eye and walked right on."

He laughed and said, "Charlie, he didn't even see you. When he's on the golf course, he only sees one thing, and that's the next hole and the next tee." And I think that was absolutely right. I've known other people who had the same experience, where he would look right through them just as though they never existed. In his mind, they didn't.

Those were tough days. Jack once said — I think it might have been at Arnie's memorial service — "I never had any problem with Arnie. My problems were with Arnie's Army."

I truly believe that was the case. But those early days were not fun, to say the least!

MARK McCORMACK

UNLIKE THE OTHER STORIES IN THIS BOOK, this story is not about Arnie or Jack. Instead, it is about a man who had a major impact on each of their lives. I am referring to Mark McCormack.

A happy group including Arnie, Marilyn, and Mark McCormack, far left.
Mark left an indelible impact on the world of sports.

Oddly enough, I knew Mark before Arnie and Jack did. He was a year ahead of me at Yale Law School in the mid-'50s and we saw one another from time to time, though we didn't know one another well until some years later.

When Mark first left law school he served in the Army and then went to work for a prestigious Cleveland law firm.

In 1960 he founded IMG and signed Arnie as his first client, followed soon by Gary Player, and sometime later signed Jack and a host of great players from other sports as well as worldwide celebrities.

There is simply no doubt that Mark/IMG was the founder of sports marketing. Nothing like IMG had been seen before, and it became a worldwide powerhouse in the sports business.

Mark and I reconnected when I became commissioner of the LPGA in 1990. He was a strong supporter of women's golf and we did a number of deals together. I found him brilliant and tough and a genuine pleasure to work with. He died at age 72 — much too soon!

Of course, his work with Arnold Palmer was legendary, beginning with that famous handshake that started an enduring relationship and friendship.

WINNIE AND BARBARA

NO DISCUSSION OF Arnold Palmer and Jack Nicklaus would be complete without mentioning the two incredible women they married — Winnie and Barbara. Indeed, the depth of the two women's friendship may have been the principal driving force that, I believe, enabled the friendship between their husbands to survive the trauma that often accompanied their intense rivalry on the golf course. If Arnold and Jack were different, Winnie and Barbara were not. Both were bright, warm and outgoing and incredibly giving — to their husbands, their family, their friends, and their communities. Barbara has said to me more than once, "Winnie Palmer was always my hero." and Winnie in turn told me that, "There is no one I admire more than Barbara Nicklaus."

Winnie … a wonderful, happy lady. *Photo by Howdy Giles*

Barbara … a delightful and caring lady. *Photo by Jim Mandeville/ Nicklaus Companies*

A great couple — beloved in the golf and charity worlds.

The King and his Queen. *Photo by Howdy Giles*

Barbara received the Bob Jones Award in 2015 – the USGA's most prestigious award. I was honored to be asked to present her for the award. *Photo by Jim Mandeville/Nicklaus Companies*

Winnie was unbelievably thoughtful. If she read a book that she thought you would like, she had a copy on your doorstep. If she saw an article in *The New Yorker* (her favorite), it would appear on your desk. Every birthday or anniversary would find some flowers or sweets or some remembrance. Her thoughtfulness is even more amazing when you consider the number of friends that she had. Her death was a tragic loss for anyone who values goodness and graciousness.

As I have said, Barbara had many of Winnie's qualities. But one of Barbara's strengths best sums up this remarkable woman. Every year at the Captains Club dinner during tournament week at Muirfield Village, Barbara presents each "Captain" with a beautiful piece of crystal, which is always accompanied by a handwritten note. This is not a short generic note that is the same for everyone, but, rather, a lengthy personalized note of thanks and thoughts that are relevant to the particular recipient. I have seen Barbara do this with gatherings as large as 30 or 40 people, and it is simply remarkable to know how she does it. Winnie used to laugh and suggest that Barbara must sleep only one or two hours a night in order to get all of her correspondence done with such warmth and her very personal touch.

But perhaps the ultimate compliment to both of these ladies is how they each raised wonderful children in the midst of the turbulent life their husbands provided them! Again, I am confident that this long and deep friendship was a critical piece of the warm and close relationship that developed between Arnie and Jack.

With this caddie (Barbara), it's no wonder Jack won so many events.

Winnie was an amazing person in many ways. She is deeply missed.
Photos by Jim Mandeville/ Nicklaus Companies

FURTHER WORD
ABOUT THE
CAPTAINS CLUB

THE CAPTAINS CLUB WAS INSPIRED BY a conversation between Jack and the legendary Joe Dey — longtime executive director of the USGA — before Muirfield Village golf course opened. Jack was concerned that he had so many thoughts and dreams and plans for his Memorial Tournament that he would need some help, and the Captains Club became a reality. It gave him a group of "golfing statesmen," as he remembered them, to help him make all important decisions. Since the inception of the tournament in 1976, the Captains Club has advised on the constitution and conduct of the Memorial Tournament while also being an important sounding board for Jack.

The early members of the Captains Club were an impressive group to say the least. Just to drop a few names, they included President George W.H. Bush, Sir Sean Connery, Bing Crosby, Joe Dey, President Gerald Ford, Bob Hope, Byron Nelson, Arnold Palmer, and many others. The current Captains Club includes a similar group of "golfing statesmen," and several women, such as Judy Rankin, Juli Inkster, Carole Semple Thompson, Judy Bell, and, of course, Barbara Nicklaus.

Both Bing Crosby, left, and Bob Hope were early members of the Captains Club. Here, Bing holds his nose as they pair off at a fund-raiser for the Navy League at Llanerch Country Club near Philadelphia in 1943. *Photo from Getty Images.*

DOW FINSTERWALD

WHEN ARNIE JOINED THE TOUR, he quickly became friends with another great player named Dow Finsterwald. Dow came out at the same time as Arnie — same year — 1955. In those days of low purses, it was not

Dow Finsterwald and Arnold Palmer in 1958. *Photo courtesy of USGA Archives*

Dow Finsterwald is loaded down with a check, medal, and cup after winning the PGA Golf Championship in 1958. *Photo courtesy of USGA Archives*

uncommon for two pros to get together and combine and split any money they might win. For example, if one won $5,000 and the other $3,000, they would combine it and each get $4,000. In the beginning Arnie and Dow knew one another reasonably well so they cooked up a deal by which they would split any winnings. But Arnie didn't do very well the first year or two, and Dow loves to tell what happened. He said to himself, "You know, this is not getting me anywhere." So he began to reassess the arrangement. "Arnie," he said, "this is not working very well. Maybe we ought to end our little partnership." So, they did and the rest is history. Arnie went on to make significant money by the standards of the day. Although Dow did well, his earnings did not approach Arnie's.

Dow smiles today when he recounts the story. He makes sure to point out that his wife, Linda, always told him that it was the dumbest decision he had ever made.

It needs to be said that Dow Finsterwald was a great player. He won 11 tournaments and a PGA Championship. He played on four Ryder Cup teams and was the non-playing captain of the 1977 team. He won the Vardon Trophy in 1957, an honor that is awarded to the tour professional with the lowest scoring average. But he was a very cautious player. Where Arnie would often "go for broke," Dow would be more careful. They were dear friends and remained so until Arnie passed away.

Dow is still living at Bay Hill.

ARNOLD AND WINNIE VISIT JACKSON HOLE

WHEN WE WERE LIVING IN Jackson Hole, Wyoming, Arnie and Winnie visited us on occasion. The first year we took them to the lovely Jenny Lake Lodge up near the glorious Teton Mountain Range. It was a very popular spot, and I had made a reservation.

So, we go in and the maître d' seated us at a table at the rear of the dining room. Then, after about five minutes, we ordered a drink and Arnie stood up and said, "I think I'll get up and stretch my legs."

When he left, Winnie said, "He needs an autograph or two."

"What?" I said.

"He needs an autograph or two."

He's gone for about 10 minutes and he comes back and says, "Well, a few people around here know who I am."

I never forgot that, because reaching out to fans was really important to him. His back and forth with his followers was unprecedented and will probably never happen to that degree with another pro golfer. It meant a lot to him to have fans know how he loved to reach out — and for the fans to reciprocate. One of the special traits about Arnie was that he could gaze over a crowd and convince each person that he was looking right at them. I don't know how he did it, but he did. People would say, "He looked right at me."

He signed autographs, as I am sure you know, endlessly. But I learned one of his tricks. One day he was coming off the 18th and I had his cart right

Arnie and I walking Teton Pines during one of his visits to the golf course, which he had designed. Neither of us could ever remember why we were laughing so hard.

there. I went over and I said, "Where do you want to go?" "Oh, go to the Clubhouse." So, I got in and prepared to drive. But Arnie said, "No, no, I'm going to drive."

So, he got in the driver's seat and the cart moved about 1/100th a mile per hour. He would deliberately go slow so he could give autographs along the way to the clubhouse. By the time he got to the clubhouse, the crowd had thinned. It was much easier for him to make his departure. I've never forgotten that. He had that down to a science.

Arnold's interaction with the gallery and his fans everywhere was something that we frequently discussed. I told him that, in my view, the crowds were his "oxygen" and he, in turn, energized and excited the crowds like no other player before or since.

He didn't disagree.

Arnie and I settling all the world's problems on the back deck of our home at Teton Pines.

SIMPLER
THE BETTER

AS I CAME TO KNOW ARNIE BETTER, I realized that he was actually a very simple, uncomplicated man — and I mean this in the very best sense. Simple and uncomplicated in food (meatloaf, pot roast, etc.), simple in entertainment (John Wayne movies), simple in books (he loved Western novels),

and simple in his love of and approach to golf. An incident that illustrates this occurred during one of his visits to Teton Pines.

While he was there, I arranged a golf game with the club pro, the president of the club, a good pal of mine, and yours truly. The president of the club, Clarke Nelson, was a very interesting man. We were good friends. He had been quite successful in business, was brilliant with numbers, and loved to play cards and golf and gamble at each.

Clarke truly loved to bet on golf. I have never known anyone who could come up with more bets in a golf match. As Arnie and I arrived at the first tee, Clarke greeted us and then laid out all the bets that would be in our upcoming match — presses, double presses, mulligans, closest to the pin on certain holes, longest drives, and on and on.

But, before he could finish, Arnie walked onto the tee, looked at Clarke, and said simply, "We'll play a $2 Nassau and you're up." For those who don't know golf, a $2 Nassau is probably the simplest bet in golf — just like Arnie: $2 to the winner of the front nine, $2 to the winner of the back nine, and $2 to the winner of the total 18. The essence of simplicity. Clarke was speechless but dutifully stepped to the first tee and hit the first shot.

Teton Pines is another great course designed by Arnie. It's especially beautiful in the fall. *Photo courtesy of Teton Pines Resort and Country Club*

ARNIE AND TRADITION GOLF CLUB

LET ME SAY A WORD ABOUT Arnie and Tradition Golf Club. For years, he would come out to the desert to play in the Bob Hope Classic. He won many tournaments in the desert, and he won "The Hope" five times! When Hope died and they moved (in my opinion with untoward haste) to take Hope's name off the tournament, Arnie began to lose interest.

Arnie and Jack had many things in common, especially these wonderful statues. Arnie's statues are at Wake Forest, Bay Hill, and Tradition Golf Club (shown at right). Jack's statue, above, stands in a beautiful spot in front of the clubhouse at Muirfield Village.

Yours truly and Arnold's grandson Sam. A fine golfer and an even finer person. We are standing in front of Arnie's statue at Tradition.

It was the same way (and I'm a little closer to this one) when Dinah Shore died and Nabisco wanted to take her name off the LPGA Tournament (a "Major") at the great Mission Hills Golf Club in Rancho Mirage. I was commissioner of the LPGA then and had enough clout to keep them from doing it for, I think, three years. But it eventually happened. Sad.[4]

As I noted, the minute Hope's name was removed from the event, Arnie began to lose interest and would only attend the tournament if his grandson

---

[4] Oldtimers (including me) still refer to the two events as "The Hope" and "The Dinah."

Arnie and actor and comedian Bob Hope, 1962. Arnie and Bob were on location for an upcoming film. Hope's love of golf spawned the Bob Hope Classic. *Photo from AGE Fotostock.*

Arnie was very devoted to Tradition Golf Club and he became (and still is) the "face" of the club.

Sam was playing. So, his stays in the desert were shorter. But he always came out for at least a month or six weeks each year.

Arnie was very devoted to Tradition Golf Club and, not surprisingly, he became (and still is) the "face" of the club. Recognizing this in a dramatic way is a striking statue of Arnie that stands in front of the clubhouse.

The statue was originally commissioned to stand on the campus of Wake Forest University, Arnie's alma mater. Two replicas have been made. One stands near the first tee of the Bay Hill Club and the other is the statue at Tradition. Incidentally, Russ Meyer, Arnie's oldest and closest friend, spent a great deal of time working with the artist to be certain that the statue captured Arnie accurately. In my experience 90 percent of statues don't look very much like the person who is being memorialized. With this statue, the exact opposite is true. It is a superb likeness thanks importantly to Russ.

Another excellent example of Arnie's commitment to the club is the Arnold Palmer Education Fund. This fund was established in Arnie's memory and provides scholarships for employees and their families based on merit and need. Arnie was fully supportive of the establishment of the fund and said, "This is a great idea. I support it completely and I want to make the original contribution." And he wrote a check to get it off the ground.

ARNOLD PALMER'S RESTAURANT

IT IS CLEAR BY NOW THAT AN IMPORTANT PART OF Arnold Palmer's legacy will be the restaurant in La Quinta, California, that bears his name. Located just five minutes from Arnie's home at the Tradition Golf Club, it has earned the reputation as one of the finest restaurants in the Coachella Valley and the greater Palm Springs area. I was involved from the beginning in my role as Arnie's consultant and advisor and as one of the original eight or 10 investors. But the project was the brainchild of David Chapman, the developer of Tradition Golf Club, and he deserves full credit for building and managing a first-class facility. Arnold was very proud of his restaurant and spent a great deal of time there when he was in the desert.

The current owner is Don Kelleher, a prominent businessman from the San Francisco area and a member of Tradition Golf Club. Don bought out the other owners a couple of years ago and takes a deep and caring interest in the restaurant. Incidentally, Don also owns a fine restaurant in the Napa Valley called Brix. Arnie's restaurant has a superb professional general manager — Dustin Nichols — who has had much to do with the restaurant's success. Dustin is intelligent, hardworking, reliable, trustworthy, and is highly respected in the restaurant industry.

One of the interesting issues that arose early on was whether we should stick to a single restaurant or pursue a chain of restaurants bearing Arnie's name. Not surprisingly, many companies, when they learned that Arnie was

The back patio at Arnold Palmer's Restaurant. This has become one of the favorite dining spots in the Coachella Valley.

embarking on a restaurant venture, contacted us. My strong advice was that we not attempt a chain, and my reasoning went like this: With just one restaurant, we could ensure that the highest quality was associated with the Palmer name. A chain would make that virtually impossible. I said to Arnie one day, "I know you and I know that if you had a chain of restaurants, you would be beside yourself when, every week or so, you would get the inevitable complaint from one of the customers of the chain about the food or service. This is something that you simply don't need. I know that it would bother you a lot and you would attempt to respond to any and all complaints." Happily, he agreed, and we never looked back on that decision.

But there is an amusing story regarding a possible chain. Among the people who approached us about building an Arnold Palmer's Restaurant in their area was a prestigious restaurant operator in a large Western city. We

A view of the interior of the Palmer Room at the restaurant.

agreed to meet him and listen to his proposal.

Before going further, it needs to be said that Arnie was deeply involved in all aspects of the restaurant — even to the point of making a significant contribution to the menu. He wanted it to reflect his food tastes and it did — and still does. He was very possessive about the menu.[5]

When the meeting began, it was very cordial. The organization that wanted to build another Arnold Palmer's Restaurant was highly recommended and made a strong presentation. When they were finished, I said, "Let me ask you this. You couldn't just take the restaurant as it is in La

---

(5) He insisted, for example, that the menu contain a number of comfort foods, the kind of food Arnie liked — meatloaf, mashed potatoes, gravy, pot roast, ribs, and so forth.

Another view of the Palmer Room.

Quinta and move the concept to your location without some changes. Isn't that right?"

Their response went like this: "Of course, we would need to make some changes. For example, we would need to make some changes in the menu to reflect local tastes."

I looked at Arnie and saw him roll his eyes, and I remember thinking that this meeting would not last much longer. In not more than two minutes Arnie said, "Well, I've got another meeting. Charlie will stay here and fill me in on what happens."

Not surprisingly, that was the end of any serious discussions regarding a chain of Arnold Palmer's Restaurants.

Two more stories about the restaurant. Arnie loved baked beans, so one of the side dishes listed on the menu was baked beans. Well, very few people ever ordered them, and they were taken off the menu. When he came back

Thank you for joining us . . . I truly hope you enjoyed my favorite restaurant! Please visit us again for lunch or dinner very soon.

Arnold Palmer

The card given to early patrons of Arnold's restaurant as they finished their meal.

to the desert one year after baked beans had been removed, we went to the restaurant with David Chapman. We sat down and Arnie looked at the menu and said, "Where are the baked beans?" David looked panicky and said, "Oh hold on, we've got baked beans, we've got baked beans." Of course, "we" didn't! So, David had one of his waiters race down to a nearby Ralph's Supermarket and buy several cans of baked beans. They stayed on the menu for another couple of months, I guess, until Arnie went back east. The baked beans were a big deal!

A second story: There is a photograph in the restaurant which, if you haven't seen it, you need to. The incident that caused the photograph did not happen at Arnie's restaurant, but it happened at a restaurant somewhere in the desert. According to the Golden Bear, the two rivals were competing in a tournament by day and enjoying the Palm Springs scene by night. At one restaurant, he and Arnie were leaving the bathroom when they inadvertently separated a woman from her hair.

"We brushed by this gal," Jack recalled, "and she must have been mortified because she had a wig on, and as we brushed by her, we knocked the wig off and it fell to the floor."

Nicklaus said he immediately picked up the wig and put it on his head. Then he and Arnie danced together to the delight of everyone in the room except, I suspect, the poor wigless lady.

By the way, you can access a photograph of this hilarious moment by going to Google and searching for something like "Arnie and Jack dance together with Jack wearing a lady's wig."

Finally, I want to elaborate on a few of the reasons the restaurant has been successful in addition to the obvious benefit of bearing Arnie's name. First is that the restaurant has a large and beautiful outdoor patio that can serve 200 to 300 people for dinner. This is a real asset any time, but it was particularly helpful during the pandemic when indoor dining was not possible. Palmer's has done a strong business during the pandemic because of the size and appeal of the outdoor patio. The second reason is the creation of the "Palmer Room," which is basically a mini-museum inside the restaurant. It contains priceless memorabilia including replicas of Arnie's major trophies, photographs, and portraits galore. Visitors love to tour the room, and it is touching to occasionally see an older person leave the room with tears in his or her eyes. Arnie's appeal and their vivid memories of him continue to amaze me.

The restaurant also has a terrific chef and one of the finest guitar players that you have ever heard, making the patio even more desirable.

THE AMAZING PORTRAIT OF ARNIE BY PROFESSOR JIM CHASE

ONE OF THE ITEMS IN THE PALMER ROOM at the Arnold Palmer's Restaurant is so unique that it needs and deserves special mention. Here's the background.

One day during the years that I worked with Arnie at Bay Hill, we had a call from Jim Chase, a professor at Pacific Union College in northern California. Jim said he had something he wanted to share with Arnold — a unique portrait that he could not actually describe on the phone, and that he would like to come to Orlando to share.

A meeting with Arnie was arranged and Jim, a delightful man, arrived at Arnie's office and Arnie, Ed Seay (the CEO of Arnie's course design company), and I sat down to hear Jim's story.

He explained that he had created a portrait of Arnie. When we asked what was unique, he said, "Let me show you."

Jim unrolled the 30-by-40-inch portrait he had created. Arnie, Ed, and I were speechless.

From a distance the portrait appears to be a pen on paper drawing of

Arnie in the '70s. But up close and looking through a magnifying glass, it is made up of tiny words, phrases, and numbers about Arnie's life and career. There are 22,719 words and phrases, and because of its intricacy it took Jim 15 years to complete!

Here I am admiring the Jim Chase portrait of Arnie in the Palmer Room at Arnold Palmer's Restaurant in La Quinta, California.

When we had stared at the portrait and absorbed the incredible work Jim had done, Arnie said, "This is the most amazing thing I have ever seen in my entire life."

The original of the portrait hangs in the USGA Museum in Far Hills, New Jersey. Because of our friendship and work together, Jim was gracious enough to give me the first print, and I have loaned it to the Arnold Palmer's Restaurant in La Quinta, where it hangs, fittingly, in the Palmer Room.

It is really almost impossible to appropriately describe the portrait. You can, of course, view it at the restaurant or you can Google it and find a full description of this amazing piece of art.

A visitor to the Arnold Palmer room in Arnie's restaurant using a magnifying glass to read the words that make up the portrait.

A PHOTO STORY

SPEAKING OF PORTRAITS OF ARNIE, here's a delightful story about a photograph. It goes like this.

Arnie's friend's mother was in a nursing home. She had a number of photographs of friends and relatives on the wall above her bed, including an autographed photograph of Arnie. One day another friend went to visit and, noting all the photographs, said to the lady, "Mrs. Jones, these are wonderful pictures and I'm sure they give you a lot of comfort." She turned and looked at the array of photographs and said, "I don't know who all those people are, but that (pointing to Arnie's photograph) is Arnold Palmer!"

A classic story and a delightful one.

Arnie always got a big laugh out of this story. *Photo by Jim Mandeville/Nicklaus Companies*

WHAT'S AN "ARNOLD PALMER?"

WHAT'S AN ARNOLD PALMER? The answer is provided by Arnie's old pal Russ Meyer, chairman emeritus of Cessna. Here's what Russ reports:

> Interesting bit of history. As you may already know, Thunderbird Country Club is the source of the "Arnold Palmer" drink. Arnold played in the early PGA tournaments at Thunderbird.
>
> Allegedly, while having lunch after finishing his round, Arnie went through the buffet line and then poured himself a drink of half iced tea and half lemonade. A woman who was behind him asked the waitress who he was. The waitress said, "That's Arnold Palmer," to which the woman responded, "Then I'll have an Arnold Palmer." Bingo.
>
> Whether or not true, it's an interesting story and the woman would never know how much income that created for Arnie.

The Arnold Palmer.

JACK'S FIRST VISIT TO ARNIE'S RESTAURANT

I GOT A TELEPHONE CALL ONE DAY from Jack, who told me that he was in our vicinity (La Quinta) and wondered if we might have dinner that night. He was there to look at a golf course he had built in the area. I told him that we would be delighted, but wondered if he would be comfortable having dinner with Arnie at Arnie's restaurant? Jack laughed and said that would be great, assuming the food was any good!

I told Arnie and he was delighted to join Jack for dinner. So, we went to the restaurant, had a drink, and ordered our meal. Arnie then said to Jack, "Let me give you a tour." What happened next was classic. You really had to be there to fully appreciate it but let me try to give you a bit of a feel for what happened. The restaurant is divided into five rooms, and Arnie and Jack walked through all five saying hello to people, posing for pictures, giving autographs, and the whole works. The people were simply flabbergasted to not only see Arnie in his restaurant but to see the Golden Bear with him. A lot of people were simply speechless and dropped napkins and silverware as they absorbed the shock. Of course, Arnie and Jack loved the whole experience. Sadly, it can never be repeated.

The entrance to Arnold Palmer's Restaurant — five minutes from his home at Tradition Golf Club.

HOW WE ENDED UP AT TRADITION

MARILYN AND I WERE COMING TO THE DESERT one year where I was going to play in the Pro-Am at "The Dinah." Arnie said, "I want you to stop by a club named Tradition where I just built a golf course. I think, Charlie, it is one of the best courses I have ever built."

So, sure enough, we did. We came to Tradition, met the developer, David Chapman, and did a little tour. Not surprisingly, by the end of the day, we'd bought a lot right next to Arnie's. Arnie and I commissioned the building of casitas with the same builder. I remember having a conversation with the builder, and I said, "Now look, be sure and finish Arnie's house first. I don't want to have to explain to him why our house is finished before his." And happily they did.

When we were living next door, I would take him a Starbucks every morning and we would have a Ketel One — or two or three — every night. Ketel One vodka was an Arnold Palmer sponsor. I remember one morning when I took him a Starbucks and we sat down to visit. One of the first things he always did was look at the golf scores for the day before. I peeked over his shoulder and said, "Arnie, I don't know any of these guys anymore." He said, "I don't either." The young guys came on in a hurry.

In the evening at 5 p.m., Marilyn and I were expected to be at Arnie and Kit's to have a drink. (Kit and Arnie were married in 2005.) Many people don't know, but Arnie was unbelievably punctual. If we weren't at his home

An aerial view of the clubhouse and the old Hacienda at Tradition Golf Club.
Photo by Couldbetheday

by 5:05 p.m., he would call and say, "Where are you? What's going on?" We would go over and enjoy a Ketel One.

That reminds me of one of the funniest things that ever happened in that respect. A member of Tradition and a very close friend of mine, Dan Dutton, came to me one day and said, "Charlie, I'd love to have a drink with Arnold." I said, "Well, come down about 4:30 p.m. and we'll have a drink." So Dan shows up right at 4:30. Arnie was sitting at his little table in the den and he said, "Dan, glad to see you. What would you like to drink?" Dan was very much into wine and, indeed, was one of the owners of an excellent winery.

The 18th fairway and green at Tradition Golf Club.
Photo by Couldbetheday

He replied to Arnie by saying, "I think I'd like a merlot." Arnie kept staring at him and in a loud voice said, "I SAID, WHAT DO YOU WANT TO DRINK?" And Dan sat up straight and said, "Oh, I'll have a Ketel One." If ever a client was loyal to a sponsor, Arnie was loyal to Ketel One.

The 17th hole at Tradition. The tee box is on the top of the mountain.
Photo by Couldbetheday

LADY, DO YOU KNOW HOW LUCKY YOU ARE?

I'VE ALWAYS LOVED THIS STORY, which Kit Palmer relishes telling. They got married in Hawaii in 2005 when Arnie was there playing in a tournament. I had said to Arnie long before their trip, "Now look, before you get married, let me know because I will need to prepare the necessary legal papers." And

A friend took this snapshot of Arnie and Kit celebrating their marriage in Hawaii.

so, one day I get this phone call. "Hey, it's Arnie, we're having a great time in Hawaii." And just because of the way it all sounded, I said, "Did you get married?" And he said, "Yeah."

But the wonderful part of the story is that they found a justice of the peace way out in the wilds of Hawaii, and they drove out to see her. She was a little Japanese lady, and as they were going into her tiny home, Kit says she said to Arnie, "Now Arnie, remember we're in the middle of nowhere and she's not going to know who you are, so don't be offended." Anyway, nothing happened, and she married them. As they walked out the door, the justice of the peace said, "Lady, do you know how lucky you are?"

Arnie smiled. His fame had reached the four corners of the world!

Kit and Arnie having a big laugh about the Hawaiian
Justice of the Peace's comments.

SECOND PLACE?
NO WAY

YOU MAY REMEMBER THAT THERE WAS A PLAYER who layed-up at the Masters some years ago on, I think, both holes 13 and 15. He was leading the tournament at the time, but by laying-up on 13 and 15, he lost.

Strength and determination — his hallmark!
Photo by Howdy Giles

He didn't do anything wrong, he just didn't get the birdie or eagle that he needed. So, we're having lunch one day, shortly after this, and I said, "Arnie, did you watch so-and-so lay-up?" "Yeah." I said, "Did you ever lay-up at 13 or 15?" And he looked at me and said, "You know how many times I've come in second at Augusta?" I said, "No, I don't." He said, "Neither do I." I thought that was one of the really great lines. Second was not a part of his vocabulary. Although, having said that, he was really not a reckless player. He was innovative and he was bold, but I don't think I ever saw him just take a dumb shot.

The 13th hole at Augusta National Golf Club in Augusta, Georgia. *Photo by Stephen Munday, Getty Images.*

Dancing with delight, Jack Nicklaus and his caddie celebrate the birdie on the 15th hole, as Nicklaus staved off a last-ditch charge by Tommy Jacobs to win the 1966 Masters Tournament. *Photo from the Bettmann Collection via Getty Images*

ARNOLD'S 80TH BIRTHDAY

SEPT. 10, 2009, WAS A MEMORABLE DAY. It was the 80th birthday of one of the greatest sports figures in history — Arnold Palmer. Naturally, parties and events were planned, particularly in Latrobe, Pennsylvania, his home, and in Orlando, Florida, where he spent his winters at the Bay Hill Club for many years.

I had the great privilege of attending the two-day party. The evening of the first day was hosted by PNC, the large banking concern headquartered in Pittsburgh, and its charismatic chairman Jim Rohr. The function was held in the Hall of Fame Room at the Pittsburgh Pirates Baseball Stadium and it was a delightful affair. The highlight of the evening, at least for me, was when Jim Nantz, the acclaimed CBS sportscaster, interviewed Arnie. They sat on a stage in two armchairs with a small table between them. Now, everyone who knows anything about Arnie knows that he enjoys his Kettle One Vodka on the rocks with a wedge of lemon. Apparently when he left his seat to go to the stage to join Nantz, he neglected to bring his drink with him.

After Jim had been asking Arnie questions for 15 minutes or so, Jim said, "King, how are you doing?" Arnie looked at the table between them and even though it contained two glasses of water, Arnie said, "Well, I'm OK but I feel a little like I'm in the middle of the Sahara Desert!" After a brief moment when we were all trying to figure out what he meant by his comment, it dawned on us that he was referring to not having a glass of Kettle One on the rocks with a wedge of lemon. It was immediately brought to quench his Sahara Desert thirst.

Arnie enjoyed a variety of celebrations to mark his 80th birthday. Here he was surprised by the Pirate Parrot and a birthday cake in his seat behind home plate during a baseball game between the Pittsburgh Pirates and Chicago Cubs two days before the big day. *Photo from The Associated Press.*

SOME CADDIE!

ANOTHER STORY I LOVE HAS TO DO WITH a very unusual caddie that Arnie had one day. For many years, Ed Seay ran Arnie's golf course-design business. He was a big, outgoing ex-Marine and loved life. He was also a

Arnie takes a tour of Harding Park Golf Course in San Francisco with Ed Seay. Here, they look over plans for the 14th green. *Photo by Michael Macor/The San Francisco Chronicle Photo via Getty Images*

fine golf course designer and partnered well with Arnie in the course design business.

However, Ed had an unfulfilled dream. He'd always wanted to caddie for Arnie in an event. He badgered Arnie over the years until finally, during a Pro-Am, Arnie said, "OK Ed, you can carry the bag today."

As Ed told the story (and he loved to tell it), Arnie hit a good drive down the middle of the fairway. When they got to the ball, Arnie wanted to know the distance to the hole, so he said, "How far do we have, Ed?" Ed replied, "About 150 yards, boss." Arnie stood quietly with his arms folded, and in about 10 seconds repeated the question, "How far do we have, Ed?" Ed was puzzled that Arnie had asked the same question again, but gave the same answer. "We've got about 150 yards, boss." Arnie then turned to Ed and with some disgust said, "Ed, *I* can do 'about'." Ed said he felt foolish because professionals of Arnie's stature don't want to know "about" how far. They want to know "exactly" how far. "About" just didn't do it!

In truth the distance was probably "about" 145 yards, but that simply was not good enough. Interestingly this could not happen in today's golf world with range finders that pinpoint the distance exactly.

JACK HONORS ARNOLD

I HAD FORGOTTEN ABOUT THIS STORY until my close friend, Larry Bohannon (the outstanding golf/sportswriter for the *Desert Sun* in Palm Springs), reminded me of it.

At Jack's Memorial Tournament in Ohio there is a group called the Captains Club, of which I am honored to be a part. The Captains Club advises Jack on all aspects of the Memorial Tournament and also chooses each year an honoree to be recognized at the following year's tournament. The list of past honorees is a remarkable lineup of men and women from golf's history; it reads like a Hall of Fame roster.

One of the rules that we always followed in choosing the honoree was that he or she could not be an active player. In 1993, when we were choosing the honoree, Arnie's name came up, and Jack alluded to our "active player" rule. But then he said, "If we wait for Arnie to retire from playing golf before we honor him, I think half of us will be dead." We all agreed and decided to waive the rule, and Arnie became the 1993 honoree. When Jack called Arnie to let him know that he was selected by the Captains Club, he was stunned and emotional. He really regarded it as a singular honor — and it certainly was.

Jack's Captains Club made Arnie its 1993 honoree. *Photo by Jim Mandeville/ Nicklaus Companies*

ANOTHER CAPTAINS CLUB MEMORY

I HAVE NOTED ABOVE THAT ONE OF THE DUTIES of the Captains Club is electing the honoree for the following year. Here is a fun story regarding the year when Mickey Wright was designated as the honoree. Mickey is widely regarded as one of the two best players in the history of the LPGA, the other being Annika Sorenstam. Once again it is impossible to determine who was the best given the many changes in equipment and players between their two eras. Like the Tiger-Jack issue, there's no need to try to determine that here. This story stands on its own.

After Mickey had been chosen, Jack — following his usual custom — wanted to call her, tell her she had been named the honoree, and be certain that she would attend the next year's ceremony. Jack came over to me and said, "I don't know Mickey really well. Would you call her and introduce the conversation?" I said I would be delighted. As I was dialing Mickey's number, I had a disquieting thought. Since her retirement, Mickey had avoided virtually all public appearances. She was not a recluse by any means but never had been comfortable in the spotlight. I thought, "Oh my goodness, suppose she turns down the honor!" When I reached her by phone I said, "Mickey, I'm with Jack Nicklaus at the Memorial Tournament and he would like to speak to you." I then held my breath as Mickey was figuring out why Jack might be calling. Mickey then replied, "Charlie, I've got goosebumps." Now, Mickey Wright didn't have goosebumps very often and I was thrilled as

Jack and I together at Muirfield Village Golf Club for my final
appearance as Master of Ceremonies of the Honoree Ceremony
at the 2021 Memorial Tournament.

she and Jack had a wonderful and exciting conversation. She was delighted
to be the honoree, and the following year she appeared with two of her closest friends, Kathy Whitworth and Betsy Rawls, and made a classic speech.

Interestingly enough just a few years later, Annika Sorenstam was the
honoree. She had asked me several times whether I thought she would ever
be the honoree. I told her I felt sure she would but that it was still too early in
her career. In her speech on the day that she was honored, she turned to me
and smiled and said, "Charlie, am I old enough now?"

Arnold Palmer and women's golf star Nancy Lopez share a laugh during a World Golf Hall of Fame press conference at the final round of the Arnold Palmer Invitational. *Photo by Golfweek via Enveritas Group*

ARNIE AND JACK AND WOMEN'S GOLF

ARNIE AND JACK WERE BOTH very supportive of women's golf. This support manifested itself in several ways. In Arnie's case, he was always a strong supporter and played in the J.C. Penney Mixed Team event. The format was simple. In one year, a full field of men's pros would each choose a female partner. The next year the female pros would choose a male partner. Though I can't be certain, it seemed to me that Arnie played in this event virtually every year, and I know how much he enjoyed it. Beyond that, Arnie developed a pattern of writing a personal letter to the winner of each LPGA event during the season. The players were thrilled with this, and I feel certain that they pinned that letter on their walls.

Finally, Arnie, after some initial skepticism, became a strong supporter of Annika Sorenstam's decision to play in a PGA Tour event, which some male pros opposed.

In Jack's case, he and his staff worked with me and the LPGA to design two events that paired men and women pros in competition with one another. One of these events was the Wendy's 3-Tour Challenge, which was played until 2013. Moreover, Jack was enthusiastic about hosting the 1996 Solheim Cup at Muirfield Village, and it was a great success and very possibly the favorite venue of the players over the years. How this came about is another story that I relate later in this book.

ARNOLD, ANNIKA, AND THE COLONIAL

ANNIKA SORENSTAM STARTLED THE GOLF WORLD when she announced in the spring of 2003 that she intended to play in a PGA Tour event — The Bank of America Colonial Tournament. She was widely praised but also criticized by some who felt that she should not play in the men's event, and one player even refused to play if she was in the field.

As this saga was unfolding, Arnie and Annika did a television commercial for Callaway at the Tradition Golf Club. I was with them much of the day while the commercial was being shot. Arnie was not sure that Annika was doing the right thing in playing in a men's event, and at one point during the commercial shoot he walked up to her and, standing very close to her, said simply, "Why?" At first Annika was uncertain what he meant, but then he repeated, "Why?" and it was clear that he was having trouble understanding why she wanted to play a PGA Tour event.

Over the next few weeks Arnie and I talked about this a lot. He was still having trouble understanding why she wanted to do it. I said I understood his feeling, but wanted him to think about it in a different way. I said, "Arnie, if when you were playing the PGA Tour, there had been another tour where players even better than those on the PGA Tour were playing, wouldn't you

Arnie and Annika on the 18th tee at Tradition Golf Club.
During the course of their day together, they discussed
Annika's decision to play in a PGA event.

have wanted to take a crack at that group of better players?" Arnie replied, "Absolutely!" This, to me, was exactly what Annika was doing, and nothing more. Once he understood her thinking, he appreciated the "Why" and he subsequently wrote her a warm letter supporting her decision. In that letter he said, "It is certainly your privilege to do what you think is best for you and the game. Just ignore all the comments you are hearing. Do your thing, have fun, and get it done."

She did play, and although she missed the cut, she played extremely well and handled herself, not surprisingly, with professionalism and composure, although she admitted to being very nervous. And the crowd loved her.

WHAT'S HE DO ALL DAY LONG?

MAKE NO MISTAKE, ARNIE AND JACK were different in some ways, perhaps most notably in their approach to golf as they grew older. No one has ever loved the game more than Arnie, and it was a rare day when he didn't either play or hit balls. Jack, on the other hand, played golf, I believe, for the competitive high that it gave him and, once he no longer felt he was competitive, he began to play less and less. Today, he plays very little but seems to do quite well when he does — witness how he and Tom Watson stayed wealthy on their winnings each year in the Senior Skins Game!

Let me tell you my favorite story that illustrates the difference between Arnie and Jack in this respect. When I was working with Arnie at Bay Hill, I continued to maintain a close relationship with Jack, and one day went to his office in North Palm Beach to discuss a matter. The first thing Jack asked was, "How is Arnie?" I said that he was fine and then Jack asked, "Does he really play golf *every* day?" I replied that he did. Jack just shook his head. When I got back to my Bay Hill office the next day and told Arnie I had spent some time with Jack, his first question was, "How is he doing?" I said that he seemed to be doing fine. Arnie said, "Is he playing any golf?" And I said, "Not much." And then Arnie looked at me in all seriousness and said, "Then what in the world does he do all day long?"

Understand that neither was being critical of the other. They simply had totally different perspectives!

Jack with course plans during a photo shoot in his office at The Nicklaus Companies in Golden Bear Plaza. *Photo by Ben Van Hook /Sports Illustrated via Getty Images*

UNITED STATES GOLF ASSOCIATION (USGA) HONORS ARNIE AND JACK

ONE DAY WE GOT A CALL FROM three gentlemen from the USGA — one of whom was my good friend Fred Ridley, who's now chairman of Augusta National. Another was Buzz Taylor, a close friend of Arnie's and, if memory serves me right, was then president of the USGA. They asked for a meeting with Arnie. We had no idea what they wanted to talk about. Arnie said to me, "I want you to sit in and hear what they have in mind." So, they arrived, and after a few pleasantries, they said, "Arnold, we are about to name the USGA Museum at Far Hills, New Jersey, and we want to name it after you." Arnold was just overwhelmed! This is the ultimate honor from the top golf organization in the world. He really teared up and he looked at them and said, "I just can't tell you how this makes me feel. Let me put it this way. I feel like I just won another Open."

We all got that. He was deeply honored.

An interesting and amusing slant on Arnie's award came in a statement from the USGA that reads as follows:

The USGA Museum

The Congressional Gold Medal historically recognizes those "who have performed an achievement that has an impact on American history and culture that is likely to be recognized as a major achievement in the recipient's field long after the achievement."

Palmer turns 83 (on Sept. 10) but his accomplishments and impact on golf are ongoing. His long relationship with the USGA includes three championships (1954 U.S. Amateur, 1960 U.S. Open, 1981 U.S. Senior

Open) and the 1971 Bob Jones Award, the association's highest honor. Palmer has also been the honorary chairman of the USGA Members Program since its inception in 1975.

Another word that could be used to describe Palmer: prescient. In 2005, the USGA announced that upon completion of a major expansion project, it would call its museum the USGA Museum and Arnold Palmer Center for Golf History and include a permanent exhibit containing artifacts from Palmer's life and career. Palmer was asked at the accompanying news conference whether the museum honor put him "one up" on Nicklaus, against who he has competed on the course, in the course design field. and in numerous business ventures over decades.

Palmer laughed, then replied, "Well, Jack's 10 years younger than I am and in 10 years they'll do another room here for Jack, and they should. That's the way it's been all these years, these last 40 years. I precede him but he's close behind."

Earlier this year, the USGA announced that it would break ground on a Jack Nicklaus Room in its Far Hills Museum, with a scheduled completion date of 2015, exactly 10 years on from Palmer's prediction. In April, the House of Representatives took the first step in awarding Nicklaus the Congressional Gold Medal by passing a bill supporting the measure.

Another word that could be used to describe Palmer: grace. The late actor Jack Lemmon once told a friend that "The King" had that elusive quality. "Think about what that word means to you," Lemmon said. "I'll bet you can't say that about five friends you have."

THE KING & THE BEAR
GOLF COURSE

TIM FINCHEM, WHO WAS the commissioner of the PGA Tour at the time this story happened, called me one day. He said, "Charlie, I really need your help." I laughed and said, "Tim this is an historic moment for the commissioner of the PGA Tour to call the commissioner of the LPGA and say, 'I really need your help.' I can't wait to hear it." He said, "I've been trying to

Arnie, Tim Finchem, and me. Arnie and Tim were very close.

The King & The Bear Clubhouse.

The entrance to The King & The Bear Clubhouse.
Photo courtesy of the PGA Tour

convince Arnie and Jack to build, together, a course at the World Golf Hall of Fame in St. Augustine. It will be called 'The King & The Bear.' They won't do it. They've got all kinds of excuses. Would you give it a try because you know them both well?" "I'll give it a try," I said.

So, I talked to Arnie. "Oh no, I haven't got the time, blah, blah, blah," he said.

Jack said the same. "You know we have a totally different design approach," Jack said.

I made a couple of trips both ways from Orlando to North Palm Beach without success, but finally I had a brainstorm. I drove down to Jack's office and made another appeal.

"Jack, this is the last time I'm going to bring this up, but would you and

Arnie and Jack at an on-site visit during construction of The King & The Bear golf course.

Arnie please just collaborate on this? This is going to be a great facility right at the World Golf Hall of Fame."

He mumbled a few words that were not encouraging.

I got up to leave and I said, "Well OK, I'm done trying. Just be prepared to enjoy the Player-Trevino Course."

"WHAT?" shouted Jack.

I used the same thing on Arnie the next day with the same result. They practically had shovels in the ground the next week, and The King & The Bear became a reality. It is a fine golf course that almost was never built.

Of course, I had no idea that there would ever be a Player-Trevino Course, but it would have been a logical step for the tour to take if Arnie and Jack would not do the course. Anyway, the brainstorm paid off.

DUEL IN THE SUN

I HAVE MENTIONED THAT THE NAMES OF MEMBERS of the Captains Club at Muirfield Village read like a Hall of Fame of golf players and executives. The one exception is me. I once said to the group how honored I was to be in such illustrious company and that as I looked around the room, I realized that I was the only one in the room I'd never heard of before!

Every year at dinner we would have a wide-ranging conversation about golf, politics, and all the rest. One year, Jack's talented and trusted colleague,

Spectators watch the action as Watson and Nicklaus "Duel in the Sun."
Photo by Peter Dazeley/Getty Images

Tom Watson marches ahead of Jack Nicklaus off the 14th tee during the final round of the 1977 Open Championship on the Ailsa Course at Turnberry on July 9, 1977, in Turnberry, Scotland. At left is Jack's long-time caddie, Angelo Argea. *Photo by Peter Dazeley/Getty Images*

Andy O'Brien, came around the table and whispered in my ear that that week was an anniversary of the "Duel in the Sun," the classic match between Jack and Tom Watson at Turnberry in 1977. Tom, by the way, is also a member of the Captains Club and was seated just across the table. Andy wondered whether I would like to remind the group that this was a special anniversary and ask Jack if he would like to say a word. Remembering that Jack had lost the match by one stroke to Tom, I said, "Andy, I'm not going to say a word unless Jack is comfortable with my doing so." He went back around the table and whispered to Jack and came back and said to me, "Jack is fine with it."

So, I said, "Ladies and gentlemen, this week is special because it is the anniversary of the Duel in the Sun, and we are blessed to have the participants in that remarkable event here in the same room. Jack, would you like to say a word?"

Jack quickly said, "I lost." He smiled and everyone in the room laughed.

Tom then spoke up. "Well, I won, and I will talk about it as long as you wish!"

More laughter.

What resulted was a memorable and emotional discussion about what has come to be known as the greatest golf match ever played.

Jack, left, and Tom Watson lend each other support at Turnberry. It's a remarkable photograph showing their respect and love for one another, even in the heat of the battle. *Photo by R&A/Getty Images*

JACK AND BARBARA AND THE SOLHEIM CUP

AFTER THE SOLHEIM CUP AT THE GREENBRIER, I had a meeting with Karsten, Louise, and John Solheim to critique the event. Everybody was extremely pleased with how it all turned out, and we all expressed our admiration for the way the Greenbrier welcomed and treated everyone involved. We all agreed that the Greenbrier is the finest resort of its kind in the world. The Solheims then asked me where I thought the next Cup should be played and I think my answer surprised them. I said, "If the Solheim Cup is to ever reach its full potential, it must be played on a world-class golf course and, although the Greenbrier course is excellent, it is not generally recognized as a world-class course."

The Solheims asked what my suggestion would be and without hesitation I said Muirfield Village in Dublin, Ohio — Jack's great course and the course on which one of the finest PGA Tour events is held each year, the Memorial.

They then asked me what the next step would be, and I responded that only Jack Nicklaus could make that decision and that I would be pleased to speak with him about it. They encouraged me to do so.

After I left the meeting, I remember thinking to myself, "Boy, have you done it now. You have no idea how Jack will react, but you are committed to trying to make it happen."

I wanted to approach Jack alone and waited for the opportunity to do that. Sometime later I was flying somewhere on his airplane with him, and we had a quiet moment together. I had given a great deal of thought as to how to approach this issue and I had six or seven reasons why Muirfield Village would be perfect. When our quiet moment arrived, I said, "Jack, I have something important I need to ask you. Please don't respond immediately. You will want to give it some thought." Typical of Jack, he answered, "What are you talking about? Just tell me what you want." I then said I thought the next Solheim Cup should be played at Muirfield Village. I held my breath. Jack looked at me impatiently and said, "I think that's a great idea, let's do it."

I was completely stunned. I said something like, "Jack, I had six or seven reasons to convince you that this was a good move." Jack laughed and said, "You can save your reasons — let's do it." And that's what we did, and it was a major success in every way. Big crowds, great golf, and a spectacular golf course. Indeed, the players loved it, and I heard from many of them that they thought it was the greatest venue on which the Cup had ever been played. Jack and Barbara were phenomenal hosts, and it all turned out much simpler and better than I ever suspected.

USA wins the Solheim Cup at Muirfield.

JACK AND BARBARA'S 80TH BIRTHDAY CELEBRATIONS

JACK'S ORGANIZATION put together a wonderful montage of birthday greetings from Jack and Barbara's wide circle of friends regarding their 80th birthday celebrations. We were flattered and happy to be part of the festivities.

Here is what Marilyn and I said in our part of the celebration:

Jack and Barbara,

We thought you might like greetings from someone older than you. of course, there are NOT MANY AROUND OLDER THAN YOU. BUT, WE ARE!

SO, greetings and happy birthdays! We have known you for almost 50 years and counting, and have always taken great pride in that friendship. So, let's do a few more years — okay? And remember, as father time marches on and we have trouble remembering our own names, we will never forget yours, nor the joy of knowing and loving you.

HAPPY BIRTHDAY!!

Charlie and Marilyn

Jack and Barbara dance at the party. Pretty spry for 80 years old!
Photo by Tracey Benson

ARNIE NEVER FORGOT HIS ROOTS

ARNIE CAME FROM LATROBE, a little town in western Pennsylvania, and he was always very proud of it. Indeed, that was always his main home. He would always go back there, because that's where his roots were.

Arnold was totally genuine. We have all known athletes, or celebrities for that matter, who act one way in public and totally different in private. That was not Arnie. He was exactly the same in public as in private. And people soon began to understand that. My good friend Dick Connelly was a

The clubhouse at the Latrobe Country Club.

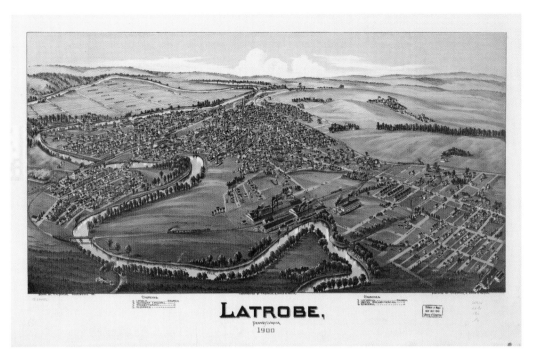

A postcard of Latrobe, Pennsylvania, from the early 1900s. *Photo from the Library of Congress.*

close friend of Arnie's for years. When I told Dick about this part of the book, he said, "I'll give you a good line to add to this section. One day when I was talking with Arnie about how his private persona was exactly the same as his public persona, Arnie said, 'Dick, it's easy to be a nice guy. You have to work hard to be an asshole.'" So true! Over the 10 years that I shared an office with Arnie, we talked privately about a host of issues. He was always the same Arnie in private conversation as public — open, pleasant, and humble.

I vividly recall one thing he would frequently say to me when I'd come into the office. I'd go over something with him and he'd say, "Charlie, you've got to remember, I'm not too smart." And I'd say, "Arnold, everyone who's ever said that to me, I put my hand on my wallet immediately." The point: People who say they're not too smart are probably a lot smarter than you are.

A similar line that Arnie used a lot was a question: "Charlie, am I running out of money?"

I assured him that he continued to have "ample" resources — to say the least.

The historic covered bridge on the Latrobe golf course.

JACK, LIKE ARNIE, ALSO NEVER FORGOT WHERE HE CAME FROM

JACK WAS BORN IN COLUMBUS, OHIO, and attended Ohio State University. Columbus and Dublin, Ohio (a suburb of Columbus), have always

The magnificent 18th hole and clubhouse at Muirfield Village as it looks today. Jack has been constantly improving and upgrading both the course and the clubhouse. *Photo by Jim Mandeville/Nicklaus Companies*

A lasting tribute to Jack in his hometown. *Photo by Barbara Hartley / Nicklaus Museum.*

been a very important part of his and Barbara's life. He built his world class course — Muirfield Village — on land that he had hiked and hunted on as a youngster. He and Barb continue to own a home at Muirfield Village, and Jack spends a significant amount of time each year looking after the golf course.

The Jack Nicklaus Museum is located in the heart of the Ohio State campus and is very much worth a visit if you are in the vicinity.

Jack learned to play golf at the famous Scioto Country Club in Upper Arlington (Columbus), where he worked with Jack Grout, the only coach Jack ever had. Jack Grout was a simple, unassuming man, and he knew Jack's

The Jack Nicklaus Museum on the Ohio State campus. *Photo by Barbara Hartley / Nicklaus Museum.*

swing totally, because he had been Jack's teacher since Jack was 12 years old. Amusingly, Jack Grout taught Jack how to keep his head still through the swing. He'd stand in front of him and, as Jack swung, he'd grab a hunk of Jack's hair so that he couldn't raise his head.

This is an appropriate time to comment briefly on golf instructors and coaches. I think it's worth remembering that neither Jack nor Arnie had anything approaching the current golfer-instructor relationship. Arnie never had an instructor other than his father. Jack used Jack Grout sparingly — only when needed. Jack told me that when he was having an issue, he'd call Grout, who would come to wherever Jack was playing, watch him swing two or three times, correct any flaws that he saw, and leave. I'm sure others will argue with me about the need for a personal full-time instructor, but I rest my case on the Arnie and Jack examples.

I also don't think it is a coincidence that both Arnie and Jack grew up in the Midwest. That is why they were so similar in so many ways. They shared solid Midwestern values. Perhaps it was my shared Midwestern roots and values as well that helped solidify and nurture my deep and lasting friendship with both Arnie and Jack. Something we all had in common.

One of many spectacular holes at Muirfield Village Golf Club.
This is #5. *Photo by Jim Mandeville / Nicklaus Companies.*

MY FIRST ROUND AT MUIRFIELD VILLAGE GOLF COURSE

AS MUIRFIELD VILLAGE GOLF CLUB was about to open in 1974, I was naturally eager to play it. Although the golf course itself was open, there were very few support facilities. For example, a temporary clubhouse and pro shop were, as I best remember, adjacent to the sixth tee.

I talked to Jack and told him that I was going to be playing with a couple of other friends, and he made the necessary arrangements. He asked me to call him after we had played and give him our impressions. A couple of the members of my group were excellent golfers. One of them was a man named Howard Morgens who was then CEO of Procter & Gamble and had a single-digit handicap.

We played the course and found it everything we had expected — and more. Even in that early stage it was amazingly well groomed. The course was difficult but fair, and it certainly helped if you could fashion your approach shots to be high and soft as they landed on the greens.

We enjoyed ourselves immensely, and I couldn't wait to call Jack and report. When I told him how much we enjoyed our round and how great we thought the golf course was, he asked if there was anything in particular that we had to offer. I said, "Jack, I would only note that, when playing this

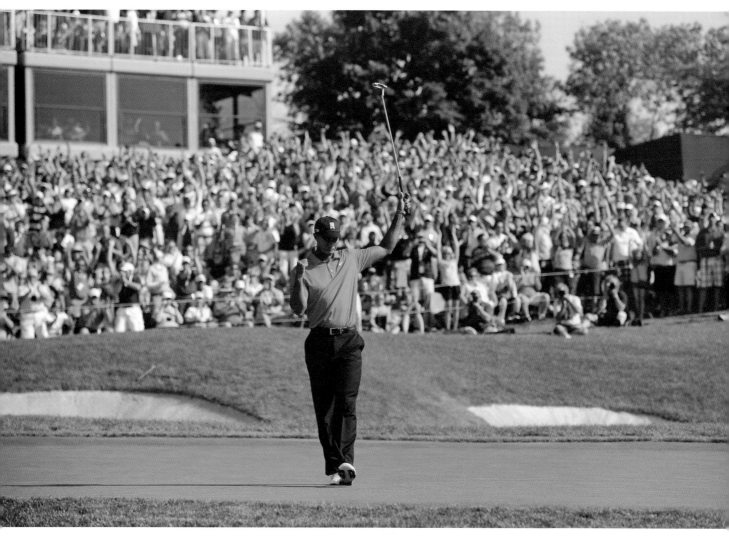

Muirfield Village Golf Club, which launched in 1974, quickly grew famous through the years. Here, Tiger Woods reacts on the 18th green after winning the Memorial Tournament on June 3, 2012. *Photo by Chris Condon/PGA Tour*

incredible golf course, it helps tremendously if you can fade a high 2-iron!" We both had a good laugh.

This was in 1974, and the course has only gotten greater and greater. Golf Digest has ranked it 14th in the U.S., although in my view, it should be in the top five. It's difficult but fair and is conditioned as well as any course on the Tour schedule, including Augusta.

JACK AND THE CAMARGO CLUB

THE CAMARGO CLUB NEAR CINCINNATI, OHIO, is a 1925 Seth Raynor gem.[6] It is regularly listed in the top 40 or 50 classic clubs in the world. I have been a member there since 1968 and can attest to the fact that it is a true classic. Pete Dye often said that it was one of his favorite courses in the United States. Indeed, in his delightful book, *Bury Me in a Pot Bunker*, he states the following:

> "When I am asked to name the finest examples of golf course design in the United States (other than mine) I always include Pinehurst No. 2, Pine Valley, Seminole, Merion and Camargo."

Jack knew Camargo well because he played it to qualify for both the U.S. Amateur and the U.S. Open and had nothing but praise for it. In the mid-'80s I was responsible for putting together an outing for a Cincinnati business club and I decided to do it at Camargo and invite Jack to join us. To my great delight he did.

When he arrived at the club from the airport, quite a few foursomes were already on the course, so we decided to get in a golf cart and I drove

---

(6) Raynor was widely regarded as one of the great course designers in the history of the game.

Jack and me during Jack's visit to the Camargo Club in 2019.

him around to each group. The looks on the faces of the players were unbe-lievable, because they had not expected to see him. We reached the first group as they were about 200 to 150 yards from the green on a par 5. They all hit their shots with different clubs and with quite different results — none very good! Jack then took out a 1-iron (maybe a 2-iron) and put four straight balls within birdie distance on the green. Several people in that group were still talking about his shots years later. Jack is widely regarded as one of the best (if not THE best) long iron player in the history of the game.

But the most memorable part of Jack's visit came after the day's golf-ing when he conducted a clinic on a terrace near the clubhouse. For an admiring (and cocktail laden) audience, he explained and demonstrated several golf shots.

After describing the sand wedge's pitch and the curve of its blade, Nicklaus said, "With that you should have no trouble getting the ball into the

Jack showing Cincinnati Commercial Club members the fine points of the game on the 10th tee at the Camargo Club.

Nicklaus borrowed a metal serving tray from a passing waiter. He put the tray on the ground and proceeded to launch six perfect sand wedge shots.

air." At that point one gentleman on the terrace who thought he knew better, waved his cocktail and slurred out, "Not if you're on hardpan!" Without saying a word, Nicklaus borrowed a metal serving tray from a passing waiter. He put the tray on the ground, put a ball on it and, one after the other, proceeded to launch six perfect sand wedge shots. He then turned to the heckler and said, "Is that hardpan enough?" The guy who asked the question sank six to eight inches and was not heard from again.

My last experience with Jack at Camargo was in the fall of 2019. My old company (Taft Broadcasting) had a reunion of its senior management and, since our company and Jack had done so many things together, I asked Jack if he would join the group. Once again, he came to the reunion and spent seven or eight hours before flying back to his home in Florida after an early dinner.

As we had done on his earlier visit to Camargo, we drove around to each group on the golf course, and he made a few comments and had his picture taken with each of them. The one comment I remember most vividly came when we drove up to a group where one of the players had just putted past the pin and was facing one of those terrifying three- to four-foot putts. Jack walked over and said to the group something like this, "Over the years I have noticed that most amateurs pay a great deal of attention to the line of the putt but don't think much about pace. They should think more about pace so that you don't end up with those impossible three- to four-foot putts. I'm not suggesting that you lag, but I believe that if you think

Welcoming Jack to the Taft Broadcasting Company reunion at the Camargo Club.

more about pace you will find that if you miss the putt, the putt back will be very makeable."

This was such a simple observation and I had never thought of it before. But I certainly agree with his comments, particularly because he was one of the greatest putters — if not the greatest — in the history of the game, and you needed to listen to him when he gave advice!

One more word on this subject. The changes in balls and equipment have drastically altered the game and, in my opinion, not for the better. To me, at least, watching a player hit a magnificent 1- or 2-iron (or, God forbid, a driving iron) is one of the sweetest shots in golf. Just remember Ben Hogan's memorable 1-iron at Merion in the 1950 U.S. Open or Jack's spectacular 1-iron on No. 17 at Pebble Beach in the 1972 U.S. Open, where the ball looked as though it was coming right into the camera lens, but instead hit the flag stick.

Those were truly unforgettable shots. Despite my best efforts, I can think of no wedge shot that has made my spine tingle!

Bob Hope shows off his skill with an iron at Central Park in New York, 1966. *Photo from AGE Fotostock.*

LONG IRONS

I REMEMBER A WONDERFUL STORY that is appropriate here. Arnie once made an appearance on Bob Hope's television show. For my younger readers, I need to point out that Bob Hope was for a long time probably the most famous entertainer in the world. He was not only a great comedian, but he had become beloved for his trips all over the world visiting servicemen and women and bringing other stars with him.

Bob was also a golf fanatic and a good player. On one of his shows, Arnie was the guest and had just played in a tournament. Bob asked Arnie what club he used on a particular hole and Arnie answered, "A 1-iron." Hope seemed shocked and said, "A 1-iron?" Arnie replied, "Yes, Bob, haven't you ever used a 1-iron?" Bob quickly said, "Only once — to kill a tarantula."

This probably worked well and proved much better than trying to hit a golf ball with a 1-iron.

JACK RECEIVES THE CONGRESSIONAL GOLD MEDAL

JACK RECEIVED THE CONGRESSIONAL Gold Medal in 2014, about five years after Arnie had received his. It was a wonderful ceremony, and Jack had many friends who attended. After the ceremony, Jack invited several of us to join him and Barbara for lunch. The group included Speaker of the House John Boehner, a rabid golfer and an Ohioan. We had a delightful lunch, and Jack held forth on golf and Boehner held forth on politics. I also remember that we had Jack Nicklaus Ice Cream. Jack had just endorsed an ice cream and we all enjoyed it very much. I frankly don't know whether Jack Nicklaus Ice Cream is still being made, but I certainly hope so.

Incidentally, I had the chance recently to renew my friendship with Boehner and we talked about the day he awarded Jack the medal. We reminisced about what a great day it had been.

Jack receiving the Congressional Gold Medal flanked by Nancy Pelosi, John Boehner, Harry Reid (dark glasses), and Mitch McConnell. *Photo by Jim Mandeville / Nicklaus Companies.*

WERE THEY
REALLY FRIENDS?

ONE OF THE FINAL THINGS I want to talk about is a question that I'm asked often, and that is, "Charlie, were they really friends?" And I say, "Absolutely, resoundingly, YES!" They were very different in many ways, but to go through what they went through and come out the other side — with, as I have said, "doubtlessly their wives' help" — was pretty amazing. So, this is just a brief excerpt from what Jack said at Arnie's memorial service in Latrobe. By the way, I think YouTube or Google still has a recording of Jack's remarks. It is very much worth watching.

Here's one of Jack's comments.

"When you get to be our age, (now remember this was at the Memorial Service and Arnie was already gone), you meet a lot of people who begin conversations with, "I remember when." It is not uncommon for a new friend to walk up and say, "I remember when I saw you at the 1962 U.S. Open at Oakmont. I was standing behind the 17th green. I was wearing a yellow shirt and you waved and winked at me. Remember?" Arnie would say, "Of course there's only one proper response — "How could I ever forget?"" As I said then and I repeat with a heavy heart today, in parts of the seven decades I knew Arnold Palmer, there were countless, sometimes comical "I remember whens." And most important, more cherished moments I will never forget. They were and remain moments that provide us a glimpse into the golfer

In this April 12, 1964, photo, Arnie, right, slips into his green jacket with help from Jack after winning the Masters golf championship in Augusta, Georgia. *Photo from The Associated Press.*

who epitomized charisma. The man whose character, loyalties, and loves were unshakeable, and the caring, giving gentleman we celebrate today. He was an everyday man, everyone's hero. Arnold managed to remove the "I" from Icon. He was the king of our sport and always will be."

Now, if that's not a deep friendship, I don't know what is.

I also remember each having said to me something like, "If I ever needed a favor or needed to ask somebody for a favor or for advice, I think Jack/

Friends, both on and off the course. *Photo by Jim Mandeville/Nicklaus Companies*

Arnie would be my first call." And I guess when you think about it, when you go through what they went through, for as long as they went through it, and remained not just friends, but very close friends, and admired one another greatly, you would probably feel the same way.

OOPS!

I WANT TO RECOUNT A REMARK that I made one night while Marilyn and I were having dinner with Arnie and Kit. As soon as I made the remark, I thought how foolish it was to bring this subject up. Happily, Arnie picked up on the comment immediately and responded perfectly.

I said, "You know, I've come to realize that you really haven't reached maturity, (and I believe this strongly by the way), until you meet someone and get to know them and realize that they do better at what you do best."

Arnie looked at me and he said, "That was Jack." And I've never forgotten that. I thought, "Why did I say such a stupid thing?" He could easily have been insulted. But I'm glad I said it because he knew exactly what I meant. I really feel that way, and we've probably all had that experience.

When you meet somebody who is better at what you do best, you've grown up — you have matured.

FOREVER ARNIE

AS I WAS WRITING THE END OF THIS BOOK, I learned that the United States Postal Service had issued a commemorative stamp with Arnie's picture in 2019. What is even more interesting is that Arnie's stamp is one of the "Forever Series" of stamps. So, what we have is a picture of Arnie with the word "Forever" in the margin. This seems amazingly appropriate as his legacy endures.

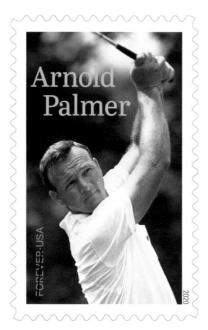

Arnold Palmer memorial stamp.
Part of the "Forever Series."

SOME CLOSING THOUGHTS

I WAS HONORED TO BE THE LEAD-OFF SPEAKER and master of ceremonies at Arnold Palmer's memorial service in Latrobe on October 4, 2016. It was held in the magnificent St. Vincent College Basilica in Latrobe, and every seat was filled. I had been asked by Arnie's widow, Kit, and his daughter, Amy, to speak first and try to set the tone as one of celebration, not a wake. Needless to say, I was honored to do this and particularly impressed with the list of speakers and how each brought a different perspective to their relationship with Arnie. The speakers included Jack Nicklaus, Sam Saunders (Arnie's grandson), Jim Nantz, Russ Meyer, Tim Finchem, Annika Sorenstam, Peter Dawson (former head of The R&A), and Vince Gill, who Arnold loved and who sang several beautiful songs. I would like to repeat some of my closing thoughts that I expressed that day about this amazing man.

"When asked what I think Arnold's legacy will be, my reply was that I think there will be dual legacies. Obviously, one would be Arnold as a golfer. The second, I think, would be Arnold as a person. He exemplified civility. Webster's Dictionary defines civility as 'courtesy and politeness.' He was kind to everyone. He made those around him feel good about themselves. He felt very strongly about manners and how one should look and dress. He

Delivering the eulogy at Arnie's memorial service, October 4, 2016.

signed his name so that everyone could read it. Maybe more than anything, he never forgot where it all began — right here in Latrobe — and he never forgot those who helped him with his career. In an age when civility in our society seems to be a distant and disappearing trait, Arnold's light shines even brighter."

My final remarks were as follows:

"Arnold, as you are getting settled in Heaven, take God to the range. Remember to thank Him for the rainbow (there was a magnificent rainbow in Latrobe that morning). Be sure He has the proper grip on the club. Tell Him that once you set His grip, He is to never change it. And Arnold, you have had a grip on us like no other for these many years. And believe me, we are

I was stunned to see this snapshot taken at Arnie's memorial service with me in the foreground. I had no idea that the picture was being taken.

never changing it! So, rest easy old pal. You have enriched and brightened the lives of millions of people all over the world. There is an old saying — "no man is irreplaceable." Whoever spoke that line didn't know Arnold Palmer. We love you."

I will almost surely pass on to that great golf course in the sky before Jack does (since he is 10 years younger.) So, I should like to say a couple of things that I would say if I were at Jack's memorial service.

"I admire and respect Jack's incredible accomplishments on the golf course and as a designer and builder of great courses. But these are not the most important memories of Jack that I will carry with me. The memories that I cherish are of an extremely intelligent, honest, loyal, and candid friend who, along with his incredible wife Barbara, gave so much back. Their charitable activities are legend and have enriched the lives of countless numbers of people. I also remember an amazing family man who cared deeply for his family and included them in so many of his activities. Jack simply did not let golf get in the way of what he considered his obligations to Barbara and the rest of the gang.

"These, to me, are my most cherished memories of Jack. The debate as to who was the greatest player of all time — Jack or Tiger — is, to me, incidental and is an argument to be had at another time and another place. The personal side of Jack is what I shall always remember.

"A favorite memory will illustrate this point. Jack invited me and his hip surgeon to play golf at the Bear's Club. Jack always arranged things so that he would lose and he could present his guests with autographed $10 bills saying something like "you whipped me." Naturally, those $10 bills never got spent, but ended up framed and in a prominent place in one's office.

After golf we went back to the house and he sat down in a big leather reclining chair and switched on a football game. Within minutes, grandkids began to arrive and one after the other climbed on his lap and before you knew it he

The $10 that I won from Jack. The words say, "Charlie, you just whipped me. Nice going. Jack Nicklaus 3-1-2003."

had six or eight kids under his arms. I remember thinking *If only the world could see this scene, any thoughts that Jack was distant or remote would quickly evaporate.* He was a genuine and complete family man."

I will end this book the way I began it: I was honored and privileged to know Arnie and Jack for many years as good friends and to be blessed for those relationships. My life has been greatly enriched by my friendship with these two men.

There is really nothing more to say.

Friends in 1965 ... *Photo by Augusta National via Getty Images*

... and pals, always and forever. *Photo by Jim Mandeville/Nicklaus Companies*

INDEX